THE
Archive Photographs
SERIES

MARKET DEEPING
AND
DEEPING ST JAMES

Repairing the road surface on Market Deeping bridge around 1910, a sticky problem for the little girls' footwear!

A tranquil scene in Deeping St James in 1930. The buildings are still the same today but the riverside railings were removed after the 1947 flood. (See River Welland and Floods, p. 87)

THE
Archive Photographs
SERIES

MARKET DEEPING
AND
DEEPING ST JAMES

Compiled by
Dorothea Price

CHALFORD

First published 1998
Copyright © Dorothea Price, 1998

The Chalford Publishing Company
St Mary's Mill, Chalford,
Stroud, Gloucestershire, GL6 8NX

ISBN 0 7524 1096 2

Typesetting and origination by
The Chalford Publishing Company
Printed in Great Britain by
Bailey Print, Dursley, Gloucestershire

URCH & CROSS, DEEPING ST JAMES.

A familiar landmark in Deeping St James is the Cross. Originally a Market Cross, it was rebuilt
in 1819 by Tailby Johnson, the local stonemason, and used as the 'lock-up' - wrongdoers were
held there overnight and taken before the magistrate the next morning. The Cross School is on
the right. No doubt the children who posed for the photographer were sitting on the Cross for
their lunch break, there was no school dining hall in those days.

Contents

MDP 62   Market Place, Market Deeping

The New Inn is on the immediate left of this view of the Market Place of Market Deeping, *c*. 1960. Built in 1802 as a coaching inn, it is today known as The Deeping Stage. (See Public Houses, p. 71)

Acknowledgements

Mr Jim Blesset
Peterborough Evening Telegraph
Stamford Mercury
Spalding Free Press
National Monuments Record
Lincoln Museum

Introduction

Market Deeping and Deeping St James are two large adjoining villages. Referred to in the Domesday Book as 'Estdepinge', meaning east fen or deep meadow, they are situated in the southernmost corner of Lincolnshire. Until recent times both have been primarily agricultural communities.

The River Welland flows through both villages and has played a key role in their development. An Act of Parliament in 1571 authorized improvements to the river to make it navigable from Stamford to the sea but these did not occur until 1620, when James I confirmed the Act and a new cut was made. This rejoined the river some $9\frac{1}{2}$ miles down-river at the lock at East Deeping. It was mainly constructed by linking and widening existing drainage ditches and was built at the expense of the aldermen and burgesses of Stamford. There were twelve locks within the $9\frac{1}{2}$ miles, each measuring 60 ft long and 12 ft wide, which enabled vessels of some 7 ft beam to gain access to the Deepings.

It was the river that brought prosperity to the Deepings in the nineteenth century, especially Market Deeping. Numerous wharves, jetties and warehouses were established along its banks in the town and several merchants owned inland lighters. These small boats would begin their journey from the riverside quays in Spalding, where the large sea-going keels and schooners from the Baltic and North Sea ports deposited their cargoes of coal, deal, pitch, tar and other commodities. Once loaded, the lighters would begin their long journey to the Deepings, stopping first at Crowland then on to Waldram Hall on the Peakirk and Deeping border and finally to the Deepings themselves. The Market Place would have been a hive of activity with horses, carts, hand trolleys and workmen unloading the lighters.

Market Deeping has a fine eleventh-twelfth century church dedicated to St Guthlac, an Anglo Saxon saint who came from Repton in AD 699, travelling by boat with his boatman Tatwin into the Lincolnshire fens. He founded a cell at Crowland and dedicated his life to prayer and religious studies until his death in AD 714. Crowland Abbey was founded in his memory by Ethelbald, King of Mercia. The stone bridge spanning the Welland was opened in 1842, forming the boundary between Lincolnshire and Cambridgeshire.

The Market Place and Church Street still bear evidence of the town's nineteenth-century prosperity with their many stone-built houses, once the homes of wealthy merchants. The properties in the Market Place now house shops, offices, banks and building societies but there are several houses in Church Street which remain as they were constructed over 100 years ago.

In 1839 the Town Hall was erected, prominently situated in the Market Place on what is thought to be the site of the old courthouse. The two coaching inns still stand proudly in the Market Place. Parts of The Bull date to around the seventeenth century and The Deeping Stage, formerly The New Inn, was built by Joseph Mawby in 1802, officially opened in 1803 and frequented by the poet John Clare among others.

Deeping St James also spreads along the banks of the River Welland. Its fine three arched bridge dates from 1651 with Deeping Gate situated immediately at its foot. As at Market Deeping, the bridge forms the link between Lincolnshire and Cambridgeshire. The history of the village begins in Norman times when Deeping St James came into its own under the influence of Richard de Rulos, whose wife's mother was the daughter of Hereward the Wake. The Wake family has long been associated with the Deepings. Richard de Rulos was a man of agriculture who enclosed common meadows, constructed embankments to contain the river and was one of the earliest drainers of the fens in the district. A beautiful stained glass window in the parish church is dedicated to him.

The Benedictine Priory of Deeping St James was established in 1139 as a cell to Thorney Abbey. Today the Priory Church, one of the largest churches in the area, and able to seat around 700, is dedicated to St James and dominates the centre of the village. It is a delight to see in its floodlit glory.

In the shadow of the church stands an ancient monument known as the Cross, built of Barnack Rag stone and rebuilt in 1819 by Tailby Johnson, one of the Deeping's renowned stonemasons. It was originally used as a 'lock-up' for those who fell foul of the law and had to await their fate until the following morning when they would be taken to the magistrate's court. The interior is 5 ft square and visitors can peer between the iron bars set in the door to view the three stone seats together with their associated chains! Another familiar building which used to stand to the side of the church was the tithe barn, sadly demolished in 1963. It was here that public celebrations were held to commemorate royal jubilees and coronations.

Almost opposite the Cross and standing in private grounds is a listed building known as the Boat House, which dates back to the days of river traffic on the Welland. Here the lighters would load and unload their cargoes before travelling up or down the river. There are two further reminders of the days when the river played an important part in the livelihood of the village. One is the oriel window situated in the property between the bridge and the High Locks; the other is the Lock Pen, restored only two years ago, one of the twelve already mentioned where lighters would have been guided through on their journey to Market Deeping. Old thatched cottages graced the streets until development started in the 1960s, when they had to make way for progress, with only one or two remaining.

There are some who will remember Deeping Feast, held in the first week of August in the field now known as Church Gate. Everything was there for all the family to enjoy, but a great treat was the gathering of old friends and relatives to exchange stories and gossip about events since their last meeting, perhaps not since the feast of the previous year. Another event was the water sport which took place on the river between the bridge and the High Locks. One of its great benefactors was Mr Waterton of Deeping Waterton Hall, the son of the famous South American explorer Charles Waterton.

The combined population of the Deepings is now about 16,000. Shops and amenities serve both communities, including a new health centre completed in 1997 and the long awaited Deepings' by-pass, due for completion in 1998. Modern construction has unearthed many important archaeological artefacts in the area, confirming its historic past.

One

Setting the Scene

An almost deserted Market Place at Market Deeping around the turn of the century. The New Inn is on the left and the King's Head is on the right. Landlord George Warrington watches the photographer. A group of four hitching posts, used for tethering horses, can be seen to the centre right of the picture.

A further view of the Market Place, with the India and China Tea shop on the right. George Linnell's chemist and druggist is in the centre on the right.

Looking along the Stamford Road from the Market Place, c. 1920. The Wheel public house is on the far left. During one of the severe floods, earlier this century, barrels of beer were seen floating in the cellar of this riverside public house.

MDP 40   Market Place, Market Deeping

The Market Place in 1956; several cars are now on the scene. In 1958 it was proposed to mark out the central island to provide more parking spaces.

Church St. Market Deeping

Church Street, Market Deeping, in the 1950s. At this time the properties on the left were occupied by Messrs Thompson, Sanderson and Hare, White Horse Inn, an antiques shop, Belton's bakery, Holland House, Dudney & Johnson drapers and provision merchants, and Feetham electrical contractors.

Church Street in 1956. The building housing the antique shop on the right dates back to the late sixteenth century. There are privately owned Georgian properties on the left and St Guthlac's Church in the centre.

Nothing to be seen on the Stamford Road in 1920, but this is almost the point where the new Deeping's by-pass will cross over.

MDP 6   High Street, Market Deeping

The High Street in 1956 is almost the same today. Welby House is on the right. The two cottages on the far left with pantile roofs have been replaced by a car showroom.

The High Street in the 1920s. The house on the immediate left was the home and dental practice of Mr Beaumont. Can anyone remember him?

The new village sign for Deeping St James, situated on the Spalding Road, was unveiled on 23 October 1982. It depicts the Priory Church, Cross, River Welland and bridge.

Deeping St. James.   R 1

Were the people in this picture from the 1930s posing for the photographer? All appear to be dressed in their 'Sunday best' which would suggest they had attended a meeting at the nearby Baptist Chapel, the tall building the right of centre.

In 1972 Deeping St James took second place in the South Kesteven Tidy Village Competition. Except for the thatched cottage, seen second from the right, it remains the same today.

A delightful picture of Manor Lodge, Deeping St James, around 1910.

The River Welland and bridge, also showing the tradesmen's entrance to the Manor House, c. 1920.

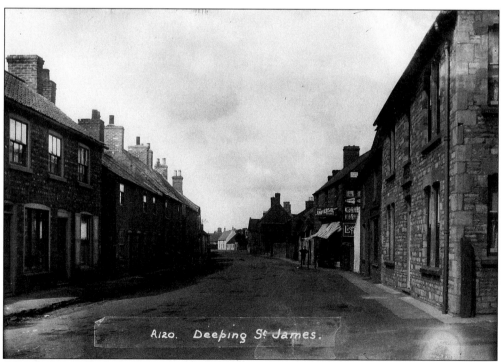

Church Street, Deeping St James, 1910. The butcher's shop on the left was owned by Mr and Mrs Nurse. Centre right is the grocery and drapery store owned by the Shillaker family.

Church Street, Deeping St James, in the early 1920s. The post office and bakery are on the left and the old Queens Head public house, with the tall chimney stack, is on the right.

This pen and ink sketch by the late Mr C.R. Burchnall shows the Tudor farmhouse in Eastgate, Deeping St James, which was owned and occupied for many years by the Swift family. Sadly it was demolished in 1964.

Eastgate, *c.* 1900. Seven of the cottages seen here were demolished between the 1940s and the 1970s. Eventually all were replaced with new houses and bungalows.

A peaceful scene depicting Eastgate, Deeping St James, *c.* 1930. Some cottages have been demolished including the one with the dormer window and the small one on the far right, which belonged to Mr Kingswood when this photograph was taken.

Two
Shops and Tradesmen

Mr George Knowles standing by the door of his general store in Eastgate, Deeping St James, in March 1926. The property, dated 1769, was demolished during the 1960s.

Delivering coal in Eastgate, *c*. 1910. Has the little girl escaped from the open gate on the left?

Mr Walter Smith's Unique Shopping Centre in the High Street, Market Deeping, in 1950. Every type of household need was well catered for here.

Mr J.H. Fromant outside his watch and clockmaker's premises in the Market Place, Market Deeping.

The Imperial Cafe and Confectioners, also in the market place, was owned by Mr and Mrs Arthur Newton, who served the most delicious home made ice cream.

Mr Feneley's bakers cart, laden with goods of the trade. The appetizing looking loaves from the Church Street, Deeping St James bakery are about to be delivered to local homes. The dog underneath the cart is taking a cool rest before the journey begins.

Paraffin delivery was a regular sight in the Deepings. Unfortunately the identity of the young men is unknown. Does the picture jog any memories?

Messrs Lambert & Kisby's bakers, grocers and provision merchants, High Street, Market Deeping, c. 1920.

Staff at Messrs Dudney & Johnson's grocery and general store, Church Street, Market Deeping, in 1943. From left to right: Miss Joan Sampson, Isabel Parkinson, Percy Tilley, Miss Winifred Rocker and Mrs Evelyn Plant.

The last trading day of the Deeping St James' butchers shop owned by Messrs Gaskin & Buff. From left to right: Ray Isaacs, Robert Buff and T. Crowson, prior to closure on 31 December 1994.

Three
Cottages and Farmhouses

Cottages along the Stamford Road, Market Deeping, *c.* 1950.

Wake Hall Farm, Halfleet, Market Deeping, *c.* 1900. Note the duck pond in the right foreground.

Now known as Hall Farm, much of the stone for this farmhouse was taken from the old Wake Hall Farm. The photograph is dated 1982.

In June 1989 Hall Farm was demolished to make way for a new housing development.

Old cottages almost opposite St Guthlac's Church in about 1910.

The gate keepers cottage at Welland bridge level crossing, Deeping St James. For many years Mrs Wright was the gate keeper.

One of the few remaining thatched cottages in Deeping St James is Osier Farmhouse in Eastgate.

This farmhouse, also in Eastgate, *c.* 1910, belonged to Mr and Mrs William Howitt who had an extensive dairy business.

The Cheese House was situated opposite the Howitt's farmhouse. It had 18 inch thick wattle and daub walls and a thatched roof. Mrs Howitt's milk, cream cheeses and curd were renowned in Deeping St James.

The thatched farmhouse in Eastgate belonging to Mr and Mrs Matthew Worsdall in 1971, prior to renovation. The thatch has now been replaced by pantiles.

Joe Hare's cottage in Eastgate in 1971. Joe was the local boot and shoe repairer. His small shop can be seen on the left. On wet days it would be filled with local agricultural workmen who would drop in for a gossip. Very few shoes would have been mended when the weather was inclement!

This charming thatched cottage was known as the White House. It had been occupied by members of the Halford family for three generations. The photograph was taken in 1971, just before it was demolished.

Six of these small cottages near the High Locks were demolished in 1976, eventually being replaced by new buildings named after the Revd Frederick Tryon: Tryon Court.

Elm Farm, Frognall, Deeping St James, dates to 1778. Mr and Mrs Peter Robinson owned the property when this photograph was taken in 1971. It is reputed to have been the Manor House of Frognall.

The inglenook fireplace in the sitting room of Elm Farm in 1972.

The dovecote at Elm Farm in 1971. Unfortunately it suffered severe gale damage in 1976.

The interior of the dovecote which could accommodate some 1,500 birds.

Priory Farm, Deeping St James, dates from the early seventeenth century with late eighteenth-century alterations.

Priory Farm cart hovels and stackyard in 1970. These have now been converted into new dwellings.

Cottages in Broadgate Lane, Deeping St James, which were owned and occupied by Mr and Mrs Fred Russell, Mr and Mrs Tom Bennett and Mr and Mrs Les Bennett. All were demolished just after this photograph was taken in 1972.

Miss Annie Jackson's cottage on the corner of New Row, Deeping St James, in 1982. After it was demolished flats were built on the site.

This cottage in Horsegate, Deeping St James, was for many years occupied by Mrs Hannah Allum. It was eventually demolished in the 1980s.

These cottages over the High Locks, Deeping St James, belonged to farmer Mr Tom Pridmore. They were demolished many years ago.

Four

Buildings

Signal box and signalman's cottage,
Deeping St James station, in 1971. The
cottage has since been demolished.

The Priory Church, Deeping St James, was founded in 1139 and dedicated to St James.

The interior of St James' Church, *c.* 1910. Notice the gas lamps on the pulpit.

The present three manual organ was installed in the Priory Church in 1970 to 1971. It was given to Deeping St James by the people of St Martin's, Lincoln, together with a generous financial donation so that the organ should remain in the Diocese of Lincoln. The photograph shows Mr Hann, the verger, helping with the delivery of the pipes.

The rebuilt organ in 1971. The work was carried out by T.L. Jubb and Son of Gainsborough, Lincolnshire.

The vicarage in 1964, seen through the garden gate. Built around 1839, and attributed to Edward Browning.

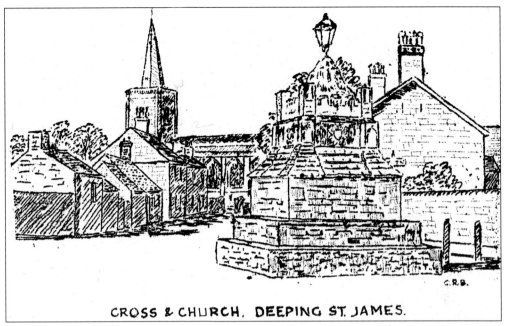

CROSS & CHURCH. DEEPING ST. JAMES.

A 1947 pen and ink sketch by the late Mr C.R. Burchnall, showing the Cross, Deeping St James, now a Grade II listed building. Originally a Market Cross it was rebuilt in 1819 by the local stonemason, Tailby Johnson, to be used as the village 'lock-up'. Evidence of its one time use can be seen with its three stone seats and accompanying sets of chains!

This Victorian building was known as the Working Men's Institute. It provided reading rooms, billiard tables and the like for the men of the village. The small building next to it was used as a voluntary laundry during the Second World War.

The Methodist Chapel, Church Street, Deeping St James, is dated 1880. This photograph was taken in 1970.

The chapel was demolished in 1989. A new one was built on adjoining land in 1990.

In 1818 this tiny Roman Catholic church was converted from a stable block by Mr Edmund Waterton, of Deeping Waterton Hall, and dedicated to Our Lady of Lincoln and St Guthlac.

The Manor of Deeping St James when owned and occupied by the Dowager Marchioness of Exeter. It was totally demolished in the 1970s. Brownlow Drive now covers this site.

The Baptist Chapel, Bridge Street, Deeping St James, was privately built by the Revd Frederick Tryon who was its minister from October 1839 until his death in 1903.

Fairfax House, just across the River Welland, in the parish of Deeping Gate, was always known as 'the Doctor's House' until the new health centre was built in the 1970s.

A delightful 1940s sketch of Molecey Mill, Stamford Road, Market Deeping.

The Parish Church of Market Deeping, dedicated to St Guthlac.

The former Market Deeping Rectory dates from the thirteenth century. In recent years it has been divided into two privately owned properties.

Old Maltings at Towngate West, Market Deeping.

Mr Feneley's bakehouse in Church
Street, Deeping St James. The
photograph was taken in 1971 prior to
its demotion.

These cottages, four in all, in Church Street, Deeping St James, suffered the fate of so many of
the old properties in the village and were demolished in 1975.

The last remaining piece of Tomlin's windmill in Broadgate Lane, Deeping St James, in 1963.

The Tithe Barn by the church gates, Deeping St James, in 1960. This fine building was 36 yds long and first used in 1299 by the parish priest for storing the tithe, which was one tenth of the crops and goods possessed by every villager. It was built of the familiar Barnack Rag stone; its original thatched roof was destroyed by fire in the early 1900s and later replaced with Collyweston slate. In 1964 it was declared to be unsafe and sadly it was demolished.

Five
Schools and Schooldays

The Cross School, Deeping St James, shown here in the 1950s, is situated to the left of the Cross. It was a mixed school with five teachers and classrooms, thought to have been built on the site of the workhouse. It is currently used as a youth club.

Miss Harper with her class of children at the Cross School. There was also an infants school in Church Street. Today there are three new schools: the County Primary schools in Hereward Way and Linchfield Road and Deepings Comprehensive.

Miss Edith Swift with her class of boys and girls at the Cross School in 1909.

A group of older girls at the Cross School in costume around 1910, ready for the play to begin.

The Infants School in Church Street, Deeping St James, was a much smaller school with three classrooms and teachers. When this photograph was taken in 1972 it was being used as the Scout group headquarters, and remains so today.

A group of children at the Infants School, *c.* 1919.

Miss Rene Hibbett, Miss Turtle (headmistress) and Miss Gladys Crowson, teachers at the Infants School around 1940.

The Secondary Modern School, Deeping St James, was officially opened by the Marquis of Exeter on 10 June 1959.

A group of pupils from the Secondary Modern School in 1968 on the school playing field. Back row, from left to right: Patsy Lansell, Linda Bolam, Patricia Mee, Angela Griffiths, -?-, Shirley Robinson and Susan Smith. Front row: Sally Moyle, Elizabeth Price, Hilary Blood, June Welby, Jane Eyre, Cheryl Moore.

A section of the choir and orchestra at the Secondary Modern School in 1974.

This new footbridge was placed over the busy Spalding Road, Deeping St James, in 1970 to enable pupils of the Secondary Modern School to cross over to their playing fields in safety.

The new Deeping St James County Primary School in Hereward Way was officially opened in 1968.

In 1980 an additional County Primary School was built in Linchfield Road, Deeping St James.

This could be the first day at school in Linchfield Road for these youngsters in 1980.

Another 'new' girl at the Linchfield school. Miss H.M. Young was appointed as its first headmistress.

Miss Pick and her class at Market Deeping Green School in 1928. Back row from left to right: J. Wass, K. Jones, I. Hayes, W. Johnson, M. Fisher, Pat Greenfield, B. Boon, C. Allam, D. Boyle. Middle row: J. Fisher, ? Turner, J. Isaacs, ? Arnold, G. Perkins, N. Roper, L. Greeves, ? Lambert, Roy Horton. Front row: Sid Smith, Dot Green, D. Burton, K. Andrews, O. Thompson, ? Josylyn.

A group of happy looking boys and girls at the Green School, Market Deeping, *c.* 1947. Today there are two schools in the village: the William Hildyard School in Godsey Lane and the county primary in Willoughby Avenue.

Another class at the Green School. No exact date is known for this picture; perhaps someone will tell me!

Six
Transport

A petrol tanker at the junction of New Row and Horsegate, Deeping St James, leaving what was almost certainly the premises of Mr Morley, whose small fleet of buses operated in the Deepings in the 1920s.

Dr Benson, a local GP, outside Greenfield's workshops in Halfleet, Market Deeping.

At the Deepings bus depot, *c.* 1920, are drivers Baker, Perkins, Blake and Smith.

A 1920s bus in Horsegate, Deeping St James. The driver is thought to be Jack Pooley.

Mr Thomas 'Tot' Hare with one of his carriages at Towngate corner. Note the village pump on the left.

These buses were one (or two) of a batch of twelve similar vehicles delivered to the Peterborough Electric Traction Co Ltd between March and May 1929. They were SOS types manufactured by the Birmingham and Midland Motor Omnibus Co Ltd who built buses for various operators as well as their own fleet, as they were bus operators in their own right. They had Brush 34-seat front-entrance bodies, although the seating capacity was reduced to 32 by the time they were taken over by Eastern Counties in July 1931. FL7513 (left) was photographed in 1929, perhaps within a few weeks of delivery whilst the second view (below) with Mr Prentice was taken in 1930 or 1931, judging by the front offside tyre which looks well worn.

A Brougham at the New Road end corner, Deeping St James, belonging to either Mr Mayes of Deeping St James or Mr Hare of Market Deeping. Both operators used to carry passengers to and from Deeping railway station.

Mr William Haines of Eastgate, Deeping St James, seen on the left, was the owner of the Blue Bus Company. He ran a service between Deeping and Spalding together with excursions to Hunstanton and Skegness between 1927 and 1934, when his firm was taken over by the Delaine Coach Company of Bourne, Lincolnshire.

One of the Reo buses from the Blue Bus Company, standing in front of the Cross School.

An early motor car in Horsegate, Deeping St James. We can see the butcher's roundsman on the far left and the milk float approaching; this could have belonged to Mr Les Ward, dairyman, of Frognall.

A fleet of ten coaches under the name of Brookside Coaches belonging to Mr Dick Wootton of Horsegate, Deeping St James. They were used locally for schools and as work buses. Day trips enabled people to visit the coast and stately homes.

On Tulip Parade day in 1981 this special, Brush 4 No. 47474, pulls past Deeping St James signal box towards Spalding.

Seven

Working Days

A traction engine belonging to Mr F.B. Gibbons of Market Deeping, with full threshing tackle, at work.

Another working engine belonging to Mr Gibbons, photographed in 1951.

Workmen at E.F. Hare's carpenter's workshop at Market Deeping, *c.* 1925.

A 1925 advertisement for E.F. Hare's products.

Mr Horace Day and sons of Towngate East, preparing to repair a roof with Collyweston slates.

69

Mr Dick Gaskin, a local butcher, sheep shearing at butcher Billy Smith's, Bridge Street, Deeping St James.

Mr John Henry Robinson, a local 'ganger', posing with his gang of potato pickers at Stowgate, Deeping St James, in 1917.

Eight

Public Houses

The George and Dragon in Eastgate, Deeping St James, was built in 1842. The small building with the pantiled roof was the cellar and the large building with the arched doorway was the clubroom, where whist drives and pig club meetings were held, as well as other social events. It is seen here in 1971, unoccupied and awaiting demolition.

The Chestnut Horse, Church Street, Deeping St James, next door to the Old Bakery. The house which now occupies the site is called Chestnut House.

Also in Church Street is the Waterton Arms, seen here in 1971. It bears the coat of arms of the Waterton family who owned it, together with other properties and land in the village, in the nineteenth century.

*The Bridge,
Deeping St. James.*

In Bridge Street, Deeping St James, stood the Indian Queen, evident on the left. Just past the blacksmith's forge is the Bell public house.

This 1950s photograph shows the Rose & Crown near the Cross, Deeping St James. Mr Goodman the landlord is standing outside.

The Rose at Frognall, Deeping St James, in 1971. Since this picture was taken total refurbishment has taken place.

The Goat, Spalding Road, Deeping St James, showing Mr Clingo the landlord on the right, with a party of friends around 1930.

The Horse & Groom in Horsegate, Deeping St James, in 1990, standing empty and awaiting demolition. To the left is the Eastern Counties bus depot.

The Three Tuns on the boundry of Market Deeping and Deeping St James, as it was in the 1920s. At the time of writing its fate has yet to be decided: either refurbishment or demolition!

An early view of the Walnut Tree, Horsegate, Deeping St James. Part of Mr Morley's garden can be seen on the right. On Monday mornings the water in the dyke would turn a milky white, indicating that 'wash-day' was in progress at nearby houses.

In 1982 the former Stamford Arms in Bridge Street, Deeping St James, stands unoccupied and awaiting demolition.

Nine
Events and Presentations

Members of the local Toc H group at their headquarters, the Boat House in Deeping St James.
Front row: Mr Truss, Fred Prentice, Bill Landan, Mr Smith, Mr Griffiths, Mr Effreys Jones.
Middle row: Reg Oldham, Ray Exton, Ron Frost, -?-. Back row: Gordon Crowson, Bob Sutton,
-?-.

The ladies section of the Toc H in 1940 on an outing to Skegness.

Decorated wagon on Rose and Sweet Pea showday in Church Street, Deeping St James, in 1971. The wagon was loaned and driven by Mr C.T. Harlock of Thorney.

Rose and Sweet Pea show celebrations in Deeping St James around 1913. This happy group was photographed on the vicarage lawn.

Miss Gladys Crowson and children of the Sunday School on the vicarage lawn, *c.* 1920.

Members of the Priory Church Sunday School at their Christmas party in 1953. The Revd Sidney Smith has his back to the camera.

Rogation Sunday at the Priory Church, Deeping St James, thought to be in the 1950s. The Revd Sidney Smith is blessing the plough.

Members of the church choir and Sunday School after giving a display at the annual Rose and Sweet Pea show around 1920. The vicar, Revd W. Pain, is on the right and Miss Minnie Charity, the Sunday School Superintendent, is on the left.

Mothering Sunday at the Priory Church, Deeping St James, in 1973. Canon Ernest Knight is the vicar. Members of the local Girl Guides and 2nd Deeping St James Brownies are taking part in the service.

The 1974 Christmas party at the Exeter Close leisure room, Deeping St James.

November 1973 saw the presentation of a colour television to residents of Exeter Close by the Rotary Club. Lady Willoughby de Eresby, with the bouquet, made the formal presentation.

The official opening of the new Deepings Leisure Centre took place on 28 February 1976 by the Marquis of Exeter.

A presentation took place in 1972 to mark the retirement of Mr Jack Lamb, centre, as headmaster of the Deepings Secondary Modern School.

Canon Ernest Knight, Vicar of Deeping St James, retired in 1971 after seventeen years as vicar of the Priory Church. Making a presentation to his wife is the late Mrs May Berridge. Also present are Canon Knight's three sons and young grand-daughter.

A presentation was made in January 1971 to Dr Charles Montgomery Douglas on his retirement after serving as GP in the Deepings for thirty-two years. Margaret Aldridge, district nurse, is seen in the centre.

Parish councillors admire the South Kesteven Tidy Village award at the Institute, Church Street, Deeping St James, in 1972. Those depicted are, left to right: John Robinson, Mr Broad, Gordon Crowson, Lewis Jones, Mr Compton (the local postmaster), Mr Bennett, Mr Farrow.

Members of the Deeping St James Over Sixties Club at their Christmas party, held at the Church Hall in 1973. Canon Knight and his wife are at the back on the far left, together with members of the Parish Council.

Market Deeping Scoutmaster Mr Steele and officers outside the gates of Holland House, Church Street, Market Deeping, decorated for the coronation celebrations of George VI.

A group of visitors and local parishioners on the rectory lawn, Market Deeping, at the turn of the century.

Ten

River Welland
and Floods

The River Welland viewed from Market Deeping bridge, looking towards Stamford in 1975.

Boating on the Welland, *c.* 1912, adjacent to the High Street, Market Deeping.

Severe flooding occurred in the High Street, Market Deeping, in 1929. This picture was taken alongside Mr Walter Smith's cottage. The destination board on the bus says 'Deeping' so it could have been one of William Haine's fleet of Reos.

The Duck Derby in 1993 at the High Locks, Deeping St James. This event, which is organised by the Lions Group, is held annually to benefit local clubs and causes. Some 3,000 yellow plastic ducks are sponsored and launched at the High Locks; the first duck to float down to the bridge is proclaimed the winner.

The Raft Race is also a popular annual event held on the river during August. The home made rafts are built by various teams and launched at Market Deeping bridge, travelling down to Deeping St James bridge. The money raised is donated to local organisations.

Feeding the swans; a peaceful scene at the High Locks in 1975.

In contrast, after torrential rain for much of September 1976, this was the scene at the High Locks.

A general view of the High Locks taken from the riverside footpath in 1958.

Boys fishing at Low Locks, Deeping St James, *c.* 1910.

This scene may have been taken during the severe floods of August 1912. The centre left of the photograph shows that the Crown and the Anchor public houses were then two separate inns.

River Welland and bridge in about 1920. No doubt the boys enjoyed posing for the photographer.

Eleven

Sports

When this photograph was taken around 1909, the May Day sports were held in the park,
Deeping St James.

Mrs I. Hibbett and netball teams at the Cross School, Deeping St James.

Members of the Deeping Swifts football team, *c.* 1922.

Deeping United football team in 1953. Back row, from left to right: Cliff Mason, Tony Melton, Don Lake, -?-, Jim Lincoln, Jim Atkin. Front row: Walter Spratt, Ray Woods, Lennie Burton, Lacy Hodson, -?-.

Members and officials of the Market Deeping football team, c. 1900.

A string of racehorses from the Vergette stables, Towngate, Market Deeping, in 1970.

At the races, with several horses and mounts taking a tumble. Some of the horses taking part were from the Vergette stables.